HORSE MOBILIZATION.

T0315699

(Reprinted from THE ARMY REVIEW, Vol. V., No. 2, Oct., 1913.)

LONDON:

PRINTED UNDER THE AUTHORITY OF HIS MAJESTY'S STATIONERY OFFICE

BY HARRISON AND SONS, ST MARTIN'S LANE,

PRINTERS IN ORDINARY TO HIS MAJESTY.

1913

FIRESTEP
Editions

www.firesteppublishing.com

FireStep Publishing
Gemini House
136-140 Old Shoreham Road
Brighton
BN3 7BD

www.firesteppublishing.com

First published by the General Staff, War Office 1913.
First published in this format by FireStep Editions,
an imprint of FireStep Publishing, in association with
the National Army Museum, 2013.

www.nam.ac.uk

ISBN 978-1-908487-60-5

Cover design FireStep Publishing
Typeset by FireStep Publishing
Printed and bound in Great Britain

Please note: *In producing in facsimile from original historical documents, any
imperfections may be reproduced and the quality may be lower than modern
typesetting or cartographic standards.*

THE HORSE MOBILIZATION OF THE FORCES.

By LIEUT.-COLONEL G. F. MACMUNN, D.S.O., Royal Field Artillery.

OUTLINE.

1. General.—2. The mobilization problem.—3. Mobilization and the law.—4. The peace establishment.—5. The Army Horse Reserve. —6. The impressment organization.—7. The military horse census.— 8. The actual horse population.—9. The legal procedure of impressment.—10. Mobilization in Ireland.—11. The mobilization of the cavalry.—12. Conclusion.

APPENDIX I.—Extracts from the Army Act. APPENDIX II.— The legal forms (Army Form A. 2029). APPENDIX III.—The payment order. APPENDIX IV.—A page from the census book (Army Book 389). APPENDIX V.—The schedule of horses to be impressed (Army Form A. 2034).

1.—GENERAL.

THE mobilization of a large Army in horses is always a difficult administrative problem. The mobilization of a modern Army in men is based on the principle that the major portion of the force is engaged in the vocation of civil life after passing through a period of military training. Certain ranks whose duty in war is similar to their avocation in peace require less or no military training (*e.g.*, doctors, cooks, bakers, telegraphists, &c.). It is only certain frontier and emergency troops that are maintained at war establishment in men in peace time.

The same principles apply to horse establishments. The major portion of the war establishment in horses of a unit is in the civil life of a country. Those horses that only carry out in war their peace trade of draught horse require no more military training than do the baker and the telegraphist—less even, since discipline is inborn. The cavalry troop horse, on the contrary, like the combatant reservist, must be passed through the ranks to civil life.

In countries where there is no horse in civil life that can be passed into the Army in war, the peace establishment of horses must be equal to or greater than the war establishment. Thus in India there is no civil population of draught horses, and the horse and field artillery stand in their lines at war establishment.

The major portion of the transport, on the contrary, as in Europe, is at work in the civil life of the country.

In Europe the artillery of the Armies only contain sufficient horses to carry out their necessary training. In England, for instance, our higher establishment field batteries have 70 troop horses. In India they have 167. The difference in cost of forage, stabling and men to tend them is obvious. The only question to be asked is, so far as this arm is concerned, can the batteries in Europe be mobilized suitably and promptly ? And for the trains, are the transport horses available at short notice ?

Now mobilization depends on two separate factors. First, the existence of the men and animals, and, second, the time in which they can be made available; and these two points must be kept distinct in our minds.

The Army and the public generally have a more or less vague idea that the horse mobilization in the United Kingdom has been developed during the last two or three years. It has been the impression that this has been due to the disappearance of so many of our horses from civil life owing to the rise of the motor. This is an entirely wrong conception. The diminution of the horse population is a very important question that demands special consideration and possible special provision. It has, however, nothing to do with the activity in preparation for the mobilization of the horse establishments. That activity, which is the result of preparation for prompt mobilization, is due *not to the decrease in horse flesh, but to the increasing necessity for meeting mobilization requirements with promptness.* This essential point must be grasped if the present situation and organization is to be understood.

2.—THE MOBILIZATION PROBLEM.

The forces to be mobilized are well known. They consist of the Expeditionary Force and the 14 divisions and 14 mounted brigades of the second line Army, with coast defence garrisons and reserve units. The Expeditionary Force has a considerable peace establishment (about 35 per cent. of the war establishment), while the Territorial Force has a very small horse establishment—at present not more than 1,200 horses, exclusive of the private horses of certain of the yeomen.

The problem is to prepare for the major case, viz., a general mobilization, when all these forces are raised to their war establishment of horses in a very few days. The total numbers required are no secret. They are as follows :—

In the Expeditionary Force, 42,769.

In the Territorial Force, 83,697.

A few hundred for the local garrisons.

Some 13,000 in the reserve units and establishments.

A total of some 140,000.

A full list of the units to be mobilized and the difference between their peace and war establishments is issued annually by the War Office, with all subsidiary instructions not included in Regulations. Such instructions include the transfer of the serving horses of units that do not belong to the Field Army to Field Army units.

The Quartermaster-General, through the Director of Remounts, controls the preparation for horse mobilization.

The mobilization arrangements for horses for a general and a partial mobilization are based on two different conceptions.

For a *partial mobilization* the available resources are—

    (a) The peace establishment.

    (b) The Army Horse Reserve.

The latter has an establishment of 25,000 horses, and is available whenever the Secretary of State for War can call out any category of the Army Reserve. It is a matter of comparative ease and can be dismissed for the moment (see Section 5 on p. 7).

A *general mobilization* of all the forces, which can only take place on a national emergency, is based on the principle that when the State is in danger the State may call on all citizens to assist it. The war footing is obtained by the impressment therefore of the citizen resources to the extent required.

3.—Mobilization and the Law.

The law asserting this principle is contained in Section 115 of the Army Act, and enacts in brief that whenever His Majesty, through a Secretary of State, shall declare a national emergency, it shall be lawful for any officer of field rank to impress animals, vehicles, vessels and aircraft for the use of the troops under his command.

This law is as old as 1692, and as new as 1912, when aircraft were added to the items liable to impressment. Between these two dates there have been additions and amendments at recurring intervals. The law, therefore, is neither an old law suddenly revived, nor a new law hastily imposed. It is a law of long standing regularly revised and re-asserted. This is an important point in view of the loose talk that is to be heard on the subject. Incidentally it may be said that no people, least of all the English, know the rules and laws under which they live—whether Imperial or municipal. The ordinary householder does not know, for instance, the laws regarding infectious disease till a case occurs in his household. We do not know the rules governing our life till we are up against them. Here, for the first time for several generations, we are up against the necessity of being prepared for a prompt and full mobilization. The laws concerning it are new to us, but they are not new to our statute book.

Therefore, be it observed, the law of impressment is not the law of the War Office, but the law of the English.

Now the whole of the arrangements for a general mobilization, so far as the horse establishment is concerned, are based on the systematic application of the impressment law by an organization and system which will be explained.

Here, be it remarked again, that as the English and not the War Office have made the law, so again it is the English and not the War Office that put the law into operation. It is His Majesty, through a Secretary of State, who puts the machinery in action. That is to say, it is on the advice of his Ministers, who can only act with the support of Parliament. Under our Constitution it is idle to imagine that Government could advise His Majesty to declare a national emergency if the bulk of the country were not behind it.

The War Office is so organizing matters that when the English elect to apply a law of their own making, the subsidiary organization shall be put in motion in a manner sufficiently effectively to achieve the object in view. The War Office arrangements are all " enabling."

Be it here remarked that for the moment we will assume that the horses of the stamp required are in existence in the Kingdom in sufficient numbers for our purpose. How far this is so will be discussed later. In following also the machinery now to be described, it should be assumed that each component part described is effective. As a matter of fact, certain components are known to be weak and to require strengthening.

4.—The Peace Establishment.

With the object of simplifying the procedure of mobilization and also the state of readiness, local casting authorities have (Remount Regulations, 1913, Chapter III, and Amendments to King's Regulations, paragraph 1236) been authorized to cast any horses unfit for a month's service in the field under continental conditions, subject to the proviso that when such horses are under 15 years of age the casting must be approved by the War Office. It is the endeavour of the Remount Service to keep units up to peace establishments (or else have the remounts ready in hand at the depôts to issue at stated periods). Owing to the abnormal castings in the artillery last winter, as a result of the new casting regulations, due to the fact that the horses of the batteries raised during the war have all become worn out together, added to the recent increase in artillery peace establishments, the numbers have been low all the first half of 1913. They are, however, at last complete.

It is therefore assumed that units stand at peace establishments,[1] and that all the peace establishment is fit for war, save only young horses and those temporarily unfit.

It is assumed that these latter categories will not exceed 20 per

---

[1] The horses either in unit lines or waiting issue in the depôts.

cent. in the cavalry and 10 per cent. in other arms. (Lest any one else should make the criticism, let it here be said, that owing to the large increase to the cavalry establishments—now 509 riding troop horses and 83 boarders per regiment—the numbers will exceed 20 per cent. for the next few months.)

Arrangements are made, therefore, to add impressed and reserve horses to units on mobilization, up to the total of their war establishment less 80 per cent. of their peace establishment in the cavalry, and 90 per cent. in other arms and services. A deduction of 20 per cent. is made from the peace establishment *of chargers* for all arms.

There is no need for any telegraphing of the number of horses unfit for service on mobilization *unless* the above percentage of unfits is exceeded. Units will leave behind 20 and 10 per cent. of their peace establishment respectively for the reserve units, and if some of these are fit rather than unfit, *tant mieux.*

It may here be pointed out that as it is recognized that the riding horse of civil life, even when in working condition, is not a trained cavalry horse, on the other hand the trotting vanner *is* an artillery or transport horse. To allow of the cavalry units mobilizing with trained horses, the peace establishment of a cavalry regiment was increased by 20 in 1912 and by 20 more in 1913, while the establishment of boarded-out horses has been raised in 1913 from 73 to 83 and will eventually be raised to 120, if allottees can be found. Cavalry horse mobilization, however, is of special importance and is discussed further in Section 11 of this paper.

5.—The Army Horse Reserve.

The Army Horse Reserve, as will be seen from the Peace Establishments 1913–14, Part III, and the Estimates, has a peace establishment of 25,000. These are horses whose owners have entered into a contract with the War Office to deliver them, or such less number as called up, fit for work, up to standard, at a price mentioned in the agreement, within 10 miles of their stable at 48 hours' notice, whenever the Secretary of State for War is empowered by Parliament to call out any portion of the Army Reserve. The agreement provides a penalty of £50 for every horse delivered short or inefficient.

The Army Horse Reserve consists of two sections :—

    (i) The Miscellaneous Section, consisting of riding and transport horses. Establishment, 15,000.
    (ii) The Artillery Section. Establishment, 10,000.

The Miscellaneous Section is only a more systematic name for our old friend the " registered horse." It consists of horses for which the State pays 10s. per horse per annum in advance. The horses are inspected by a remount officer before initial acceptance, and before renewed acceptance at the beginning of each year. The only difference, perhaps, between these horses and the registered horse in days gone by is that considerable care is taken that only *bona fide* owners are accepted, and not chance owners who rely on purchase to make up their quotas if called up. The strength of this section is some 14,000, but will easily reach establishment during the year.

The Artillery Section is a new creation, necessitated by the disappearance of the light trotting vanner, *i.e.*, the " bus " horse, from so many vocations of civil life. Formerly the London Omnibus Companies registered many artillery horses. Now they have none. The horses of this section once accepted and the agreement signed are in exactly the same position as regards mobilization as the horses of the Miscellaneous Section. The agreement with the owners, however, contains many special provisions. There are still many horses of the artillery type in the van-using trades of the country. With the object of inducing owners to keep these horses rather than adopt motors, the War Office has offered a yearly retaining fee of £4, paid half-yearly in *arrears*, for horses of the artillery, *i.e.*, trotting vanner type. To ensure, however, that owners do not merely make use of the State by obtaining the subsidy for horses that they are about to abolish, the War Office requires owners to contract to provide these horses for three years, with the proviso that they may break contract at any time by refunding previous instalments, up to a limit of £4.

The main object of this section is to help to prevent further disappearance of the artillery horse from civil life, and further to encourage owners, who will continue to keep horses to keep a type for which the War Office will pay £4 a year. The strength of this section is now some 7,000. These two classes of horse are also often referred to as " registered " and " subsidized " horses respectively.

It is often urged that, as all horses are liable to impressment, the State is wasting money by paying retaining fees. This is, of course, due to failure to realize what is involved. Impressment can only be resorted to when Government feel that a " national emergency " must be declared, and that the people will support them. It is conceivable that there may be many occasions for partial mobilization, when impressment cannot be resorted to. Then, again, while it is true that on a " national emergency " the reserve horse is merged in the universal demand, the State still derives three great advantages from it. First, it is due on 48 hours' demand ; secondly, it must be delivered *after taking over* within 10 miles of its stable ; thirdly, its exact whereabouts is known. That is to say, it can be and is used to ensure the punctual mobilization of units required early in the mobilization time table. The artillery subsidy, as has been explained, exists not so much to get a lien on horses, as to stimulate their existence. It is sometimes said, " How can £4 a year keep a horse in existence ? " The explanation of this is that most trade horses have to earn a certain amount of money each year to be a paying proposition.

If a horse should earn £50 a year to be profitable, and, owing to competition, the price of forage, &c., is only earning, say, £45 or £47, the extra £4 a year makes all the difference on a balance sheet. This particularly applies to horses that earn money on various counts during the year. There are firms in England who have as many as 500 horses subsidized. £2,000 per annum is a substantial asset to any business. £100 per annum to a business that has 25 horses subsidized is not to be despised. The War Office does not accept the full number of horses of the type required existing in a stable, but deducts a percentage to allow for an average of unfit horses. The reserve horse is *not an individual horse*. The owner merely contracts to produce a specified number of horses of a type. It will be seen, therefore, that every reserve horse is an effective horse, and no sick need be counted on.

The Artillery Section has only been commenced this year. The horses tendered have all been inspected prior to acceptance by officers of the mounted branch of the artillery.

Reserve horses are called up on Army Form A. 2035. They are taken over by remount officers, or by the impressment purchasers, as may be most convenient. Receipts are given to owners (Army Book 393), and duplicates are sent to the War Office. Payment at the price agreed to is made by the War Office as soon as it is satisfied that the demand has been fully complied with.

6.—THE IMPRESSMENT ORGANIZATION.

A system that will ensure prompt expansion of the peace cadres from the civil horse life of the country demands the following :—

(a) The division of the Kingdom into suitable areas, and a demand on each area proportionate to its resources.

(b) An annual peace time census of horses fit for military purposes.

(c) An organization of purchasing areas.

(d) The arrangement of the necessary legal steps to place the horses required at the disposal of the military authorities.

(e) The provision of sufficiently accurate horse lists for the impressment to be based on.

(f) The provision of methods of valuation, payment, and protest when the purchasers take over the impressed horses.

(g) Adequate arrangements for collection and dispatch to destination.

The arrangements to give effect to the foregoing are fully described in Chapter V (Mobilization) of the new Remount Regulations. They may be outlined here, and are based on the principle that each military command provides horses for the units mobilizing within its area plus such extra quotas as may be prescribed. Certain Commands, notably the small Aldershot area, are deficient of many horses. The deficit in Commands that are short is levied on Commands that have surplus. The demand on each Command, based on a survey of its resources, is formulated annually by the War Office.

Each Command is divided into a certain number of remount circles, presided over by a remount officer.

Just as the co-ordinating authority, the War Office, lays down the quota to be provided by each Command, so the Command Headquarters lay down the quota to be furnished by, and the units to be completed by, each of their remount circles, based also on a survey of the resources of each circle.

The basis of all this is the annual horse census, which will be explained later. (Section 7.)

Purchasing Areas.—Each remount circle is divided into purchasing areas, which vary in size in accordance with the rate at which horses are required. It is obvious that, to enhance the rate of horse delivery, the number of purchasers must be increased. In circles from which the daily delivery of horses required is large, there must be more purchasers at work. The number of purchasers, therefore, varies with the conditions of the circle. It is estimated that a purchaser in a car can purchase 30 horses a day in country districts, and from 50 to 60 a day in town areas, but this must vary with different conditions.

The Purchasers.—The purchasers are principally county gentlemen of repute, who, in accordance with the custom of the English, volunteer their services, as do the county justices, the county and municipal councillors, and the like. They are appointed by Command Headquarters, and receive a letter of service. It is impossible to put a monetary value to their service, but they receive sufficient daily allowances when employed to ensure that they are not out of pocket by their services.

Their duties are detailed in the "Instructions for Purchasers" (Appendix I of the Remount Regulations, and issued also in a pamphlet for their use). A right conception of their position is important. They *are not* the impressers. The impressment is carried out by the police on the orders of the magistracy. The purchasers serve as the honest broker between citizen and State, and are charged with tendering a fair value for the horse. The more prominent in the life of the town or countryside the purchaser is, the more likely is his valuation to be accepted as reasonable by the owner. With this object the purchasers, of whom there are some 800, exclusive of 125 in Ireland, are, as far as possible, found from among the horse-owning and land-owning gentry.

The purchaser has a dispatch box containing justices' warrants for signature (Army Form A. 2029) authorizing impressment, cheque books of payment orders (Army Book 390), railway consignment notes (Army Book 391), tie-on labels, lists of stables containing the horses found suitable at the last census (with 25 per cent. spare to cover variation and unfitness), railway truck programme, showing the horse trucks that will be available at certain stations in his area on each day of mobilization, and certain subsidiary instructions; also a pair of broad arrow branding irons. It is part of his duty to brand each horse with a broad arrow on the near fore. (The nearest kitchen fire will heat the irons.)

He is provided with a civilian veterinary surgeon (whom he is authorized to pay), and must find a clerk and as many horse holders as he requires. He is empowered to pay these 7s. 6d. and 5s. a day, respectively (see " Instructions for Purchasers "). He is also provided with two sub-purchasers (at £1 a day) for the purpose of assisting in collecting and entraining, and on the first day of mobilization £100 is placed to his credit at his own bank for petty expenses. He can get more on demand. He is also provided with forms for submitting his accounts at the close of operations.

The Actual Payment for Horses and Vehicles Impressed.—This is made by the payment order referred to (Army Book 390). It is in the form of a cheque on the command paymaster, which may be presented to that officer to be cashed, or may be passed to the payee's bank for collection. The Army Act provides that the State shall pay a " fair " price. Should the owner object to the amount tendered, he cannot prevent the horses or vehicles being taken; but he may accept under protest, and may appeal to his county court judge. The judge, after hearing his appeal, may award him, should he prove his claim, any enhancement of price he (the judge) may consider just. Here we see that the law of the land provides for the protection of the citizen as well as for the needs of the State. Should any citizen impede the removal of his horses, vehicles, or other items liable to impressment, they may be seized by force, and he, on conviction, is liable to a fine.

The Adequate Arrangements for Collection and Dispatch.—These have already been referred to. It is the duty of the remount officer of the circle to study this question in each case. The Command Headquarters will have arranged the schedule of horse trucks, for certain days. The purchaser has assistance, and authority to provide more labour as required. At the entraining stations the local resources will have been studied. The market pens, to be seen at so many county towns are especially suitable for temporary accommodation of horses awaiting despatch. The Territorial Force will often collect their horses themselves, when such are from town areas close to their place of mobilization.

In other cases the purchasers and their sub-purchasers arrange with owners to send their own men (whom the purchaser will pay or tip), or will take on local labour to get the horses to the station. It must, in this connection, be remembered that the State can only resort to impressment in a national emergency, and that on such an occasion the whole goodwill of the country-side will be at the disposal of the State. Without that a general mobilization is not possible.

7.—THE HORSE CENSUS.

The whole machinery of the mobilization of horses hangs, it will have been noticed, on the allotment lists of horses for impressment which contain a margin in excess of requirements of 25 per cent.

These lists are made out every year in each remount circle from the annual census lists. These census lists are compiled under the provisions of the Amendments to the Army Act of 1911, which provide that duly appointed military officers may enter private stables at reasonable times of day to see what horses fit for military purposes exist there. Should the owner refuse admittance, a magistrate shall issue a search warrant. The Remount Regulations provide that the owner shall first be asked to name a suitable time, and for this purpose Army Form A. 2036, in memorandum or postcard form (printed in both forms) should be used. In the two censuses which have been made under this amendment the number of refusals have been trivial, and the owners have proved reasonable on explanation, and it has not yet been necessary to apply for a search warrant. Now the actual machinery for taking the census varies and may vary from time to time, the important point being that a census is legal and is taken. For the last two years it has been made largely through the agency of Territorial adjutants and officers from Regular units. In some cases civilians have acted on behalf of the military authority, and the remount officers of circles have made it in certain areas. Recently tests have been carried out by visiting an impressment area in each command with the mobilization purchaser. A circular was sent to all owners in the circle whose horses were on the allotted lists, asking them to assist in the test by keeping their horses in, and explaining the legal position and the nature of a national emergency. With very few exceptions the owners were able to oblige. The result was that in the few areas tested it was possible to see the horses censused, and see how far they had been reliably recorded, to see how many of the spare 25 per cent. would be absorbed by misclassification, change in the stable or unfitness since the census some six months before. It was also possible thus for a few of the purchasers to see the sort of work expected of them, and for the Director of Remounts to see that they had their dispatch boxes, forms and warrants, and understood their contents. The available resources for collection, and temporary accommodation at the entraining stations were also studied. The result showed that from 3 to 10 per cent. of the horses on the allotted lists had become ineffective or were badly classified, and that there was still the larger portion of the 25 per cent. of spare, available to meet the casualties which would gradually accrue throughout the year till such time as the revised allotment was in the purchasers' mobilization box in the spring of each year.

The question of the machinery and agency to be used in the ensuing censuses is under consideration. The census is recorded in Army Book 389, which is a convenient pocket book. It is from this that the purchasers' lists are made out on Army Form A. 2034 (inner sheet), showing destination and unit. The Territorial adjutants in submitting their census books to the remount officer, mark those they would recommend for their own units. In making the allotment and preparing the purchaser's A. 2034, these recommendations are given effect to so far as possible, provided that Expeditionary Force units are fully provided for elsewhere. The census book contains the necessary instructions to the census taker. The War Office has, of course, no power to muzzle the provisions of the Army Act, it cannot mitigate the liability imposed *by the people on* the people, of having every horse and vehicle and vessel commandeered if the State needs them, but it has issued subsidiary instructions (Remount Regulations, Sect. 14.3) to the effect that unless the required quotas cannot otherwise be provided, not more than 50 per cent. of any single stable are to be impressed, while horses connected with the food trades are to be spared when possible. Single horse stables are an exception to the 50 per cent. rule.

8.—THE ACTUAL HORSE POPULATION.

Though the reduction of horses in the Kingdom has been very great, it has not yet reached by a long way the limit when it would be necessary for the Director of Remounts to inform the Quartermaster General and the Army Council that the forces cannot be mobilized under the system described, or that such a situation is in sight. The actual results of the military census have shown that we need only take less than one-quarter of the horses recorded as suitable. The number of heavy draught horses is very large indeed, and these are increasing rather than decreasing. It is now under consideration to use pair heavies instead of four light draught horses for all trains and slow moving wagons. This at once taps a class of horse that is kept in the pink of condition, and that will never fail. The total number of horses fit for military purposes now on the census list from which the impressment allotment is made is 462,919 in the following classes (exclusive of Ireland) :—

	Fit for Expeditionary Force.	Fit for Territorial Force.
Riding I. (Over 15.1)	24,959	27,161
Riding II. (Under 15.1)	14,148	34,108
Light draught I. (Artillery)	28,552	43,174
Light draught II. (Transport)	23,577	58,180
Heavy draught	52,499	145,683
Pack	2,571	8,307

9.—THE LEGAL PROCEDURE OF IMPRESSMENT.

The legal procedure to be followed is worth understanding. Almost every authority on first coming into touch with this question hastens to recommend a change in the law, but changes in law are not easy to encompass, as anyone who understands our parliamentary system will readily acknowledge. The present law, though certainly capable of improvement as to procedure, goes really a very great way in giving the State full control over its citizens' goods, in the hour of its needs.

The procedure is first that His Majesty, through any of his Secretaries of State, declares an emergency to exist. (A specimen of the various forms and warrants to be used with the procedure now to be described, is given in Appendix II.) Any officer of field rank is then empowered to issue a "requisition of emergency" for completing the force under his orders. This is Form A of Army Form A. 2029[2], and is known as the "requisition." The official authorized to purchase impressed horses then takes the "requisition" to the nearest magistrate. (The magistrates handy to the purchasers should be known and warned in peace time.) With it he presents a "demand" for horses and vehicles (Form B of A. 2029[2]). With this he produces a summary of the horses and vehicles required (Army Form A. 2034, outer sheet), within which lie the inner sheets containing the addresses of the horses to be taken. The magistrate signs the "warrant" (Form C of A. 2029[2]), and the purchaser then takes this to the constables in each district.

With the Forms A, B and C referred to, are bound up as a matter of convenience 100 copies of Form D[2], which is the constable's "order" to the owner to deliver up the horses, vehicles, &c., detailed on the order. The constable either precedes the purchaser in a car or accompanies him. The actual order can be filled in and signed from the purchaser's list as the car travels round. Now, the procedure just detailed sounds more elaborate than it really is. In the first place, the motor car has so annihilated time and space. We can picture the actual procedure in our mind's eye : the purchaser receiving his requisition of emergency, or more probably a telegram telling him the name of the Secretary of State (the one in attendance on his Majesty), enabling him to complete a previously signed requisition and an order saying when mobilization commences. Let us say it arrives about dinner time. After dinner the purchaser calls up his car and drives to the nearest magistrate, and on to the next if one be away. He then has got his "warrant" duly signed. Next morning he motors to the pre-arranged police station, where he is to pick up his constable who, on the production of the "warrant" is prepared to go ahead or accompany the purchaser distributing the Forms D, i.e., the "order" to the owner to deliver.

[2] See Appendix II of this article.

It is entirely open to the magistrate to sign the "warrant" on production of the written "demand" from the purchaser without seeing the requisition of emergency so long as he is satisfied that the "requisition" has been issued and will be in due form. All that is really necessary is for him to be satisfied that the "demand" is authorized. The "requisition" is evidence of this, but he may take it on trust and the telegram to the purchaser to commence may satisfy him. This is all a matter of peace time education and preparation by the remount officers of circles. It may perhaps be again mentioned that the Army Act prescribes a fine for all who hinder impressment of their goods lawfully commandeered, and enacts that if the horses, &c., are not produced they may be taken by force. It will, of course, be evident that if owners do endeavour to hinder impressment and actually send their animals away, prompt mobilization will be much impeded. It is essential that the goodwill of the country shall be with the State, and education and explanation in peace time is the only way to ensure this. With this object everything connected with horse mobilization is made absolutely public.

10.—Mobilization in Ireland.

Mobilization in Ireland demands some modification of the system. Impressment will take place to get possession of the hard draught horses of the towns, but as in Ireland every one will sell his horse if he can make a ten-pound note on it voluntary purchase is largely relied on. The country there is divided into voluntary purchasing areas based on a constabulary census. The number of horses required there compared with the number available is so small that there is not the least likelihood of their not being forthcoming, fit for work. A large number of the horses required in Ireland are reserve horses automatically available on mobilization.

11.—The Mobilization of the Cavalry.

The mobilization of the cavalry is such an important question that it requires a short description. The ordinary civil saddle horse is not fit for the ranks of a cavalry regiment. A small number of the horses with the regiment, however, need only be trained to saddle, such as those ridden by medical and veterinary officers, interpreters, and those miscellaneous ranks who accompany the regimental portion of the train. The mass, however, must be trained horses. With this object the peace establishment has been largely increased, and when the final 20 per regiment now waiting in the remount depôts till after the manoeuvres, have been added, there will be a total of 509 riding troop horses exclusive of any chargers or draught horses, in the ranks in peace time. There is further an establishment of 83 boarded-out horses per regiment, which will eventually be raised to 120. The boarded-out horses are trained troop horses issued to private persons under certain conditions. They may be hunted and used for any private purpose except plough or heavy draught. They are sent out on a month's trial first, and must, if then approved, be kept at least a year. The only cost to the allottee above their keep is the cost of insuring them for £40, which is £2 per annum. The present peace establishment of riding horses of a cavalry regiment is, therefore: 45 chargers, 509 troop horses, and 83 boarded-out troop horses; also some 11 troop horses each at the regimental depôts which join on mobilization. The war establishment is 518 riding horses of all kinds, and a first reinforcement of 48 troop horses. It will be seen, therefore, that when the boarders are out to the number of 120, and the present abnormal number of young horses in the ranks (due to the increase of establishment in troop horses and boarders) are matured the mobilization of a cavalry regiment will not be a serious problem.

In this connection a grievance that is often heard may be alluded to. The complaint is that civilians can get a horse for £2, while an officer pays £10. But it should be remembered that the civilian pays for groom, forage and stabling, and a boarded-out horse is required for the ranks and would, therefore, not do as a charger, since the officer's charger is to carry him in war time. Officers not entitled to chargers may have boarders, and a good many do, while officers requiring horses in excess of their regulation number of chargers may have them also.

12.—CONCLUSION.

The foregoing has given in outline the principles underlying, and the system as organized for, the horse mobilization of the forces. It has not long been built up, and is only now in full working order. It will be seen that this system consists of a number of definite component parts welded into a connected procedure. Each one of the components can be taken out and examined by itself, and if necessary improved or strengthened. For instance, if the census arrangements are not good enough, they must be improved. The system will not be disarranged thereby. If the mobilization purchasers are not reliable enough they must be improved, and so forth. Criticisms and defects apply to components and not to the frame, which is the basis of the whole thing. It has been mentioned that would-be improvers are always suggesting changes in the law. It is often urged that it should be compulsory for all owners to bring their horses into collecting stations, where the purchase would be made. This sounds most plausible. But a little reflection will show the fallacy of the proposal. There is no means of marking the horse that has been recorded as fit for military purposes, nor, of course, of preventing an owner changing every horse in his stable. In our impressment lists we only record that on a certain date there were certain horses of the types required, and that as many of those types up to the number recorded, that are available, are to be taken. There are probably ten times as many horses of sorts in the country as we require. We do not want a thousand horses crowding in to some centre when only a hundred are required. But if we do not get them all in there is nothing to indicate which of them we want brought in. The only way to get them, therefore, is to buy at the stable, or on the owners' premises. And if the horses are not in, to go again in the evening to get them. It would, however, be an improvement in the law to compel every person whose horse has been impressed to deliver it for you within 10 miles of his stable.

It would also be an assistance if every subject were compelled to send in an annual return of the horses he keeps, just as he makes out his income tax return. A simplification of the legal procedure of impressment might be possible, so that whenever the mobilization posters are up the purchaser may call on the constable to issue the Forms D. These are about all the legal improvements possible.

No reference has been made to replacement of casualties in the field. This is rather beyond the scope of this paper, but an outline of the arrangements will serve to show that the subject is arranged for. There are a considerable number of reserve units of the mounted branches formed on mobilization for the express purpose of training drafts of men and horses for the troops in the field and taking over the horses left as temporarily unfit. The impressment on mobilization provides for the raising of these units and the remount depôts to war establishment immediately the field army units are complete. This provides for several months' reserve of horses. The reserve units supply the field Armies with drafts. The remount depôts in the United Kingdom refill the reserve units as drafts go out from them. The Army buyers refill the remount depôts from purchase in Great Britain, in Ireland or overseas.

APPENDIX I.
EXTRACTS FROM THE ARMY ACT.
(*Impressment of Carriages.*)
SECTION 114.

Annual List of Persons liable to supply Carriages.—(1.) The authority hereinafter mentioned for any place may cause annually a list to be made out of all persons in such place, or any particular part thereof, liable to furnish carriages and animals under this Act, and of the number and description of the carriages and animals of such persons; and where a list is so made, any justice may by warrant require any constable or constables having authority within such place to give from time to time, on demand by an officer or non-commissioned officer under this Act, orders to furnish carriages and animals, and such warrant shall be executed as if it were a special warrant issued in pursuance of this Act on such demand, and the orders shall specify the like particulars as such special warrant.

(1A.) For the purpose of assisting the authority hereinafter mentioned in the preparation of such list as aforesaid, any proper officer authorized in that behalf by the authority shall be entitled at all reasonable times to enter any premises in which he has reason to believe that any carriages or animals are kept, and to inspect any carriages or animals which may be found therein.

If any such officer so authorized is obstructed in the exercise of his powers under this provision, a justice of the peace may, if satisfied by information on oath that the officer has been so obstructed, issue a search warrant authorizing the constable named therein, accompanied by the officer, to enter the premises in respect of which the obstruction took place at any time between six o'clock in the morning and nine o'clock in the evening, and to inspect any carriages or animals that may be found therein.

In this provision the expression " proper officer " means any officer or person of such rank, class, or description as may be specified in an order of the Army Council made for the purpose.

(2.) The authority hereinafter mentioned shall cause such list to be kept at some convenient place open for inspection at all reasonable times by persons interested, and any person who feels aggrieved either by being entered in such list, or by being entered to furnish any number or description of carriages or animals which he is not liable to furnish, may complain to a court of summary jurisdiction, and the court, after such notice as the court think necessary to persons interested, may order the list to be amended in such manner as the court may think just.

(3.) All orders given by constables for furnishing carriages and animals shall, as far as possible, be made from such list in regular rotation.

(4.) The authority for the purposes of this section shall, in England and Scotland, be either the police authority or the county association established under the Territorial and Reserve Forces Act, 1907, and in Ireland the police authority.

SECTION 115.

Supply of Carriages and Vessels in case of Emergency. —(1.) His Majesty by Order, distinctly stating that a case of emergency exists, and signified by a Secretary of State, and also in Ireland the Lord Lieutenant by a like Order, signified by the Chief Secretary or Under-Secretary, may authorize any general or field officer commanding His Majesty's regular forces in any military district or place in the United Kingdom to issue a requisition under this section (hereinafter referred to as a requisition of emergency).

(2.) The officer so authorized may issue a requisition of emergency under his hand reciting the said Order, and requiring justices of the peace to issue their warrants for the provision, for the purpose mentioned in the requisition, of such carriages and animals as may be provided under the foregoing provisions, and also of carriages of every description (including motor cars and other locomotives, whether for the purpose of carriage or haulage), and of horses of every description, whether kept for saddle or draught, and also of vessels (whether boats, barges, or other) used for the transport of any commodities whatsoever upon any canal or navigable river.

(3.) A justice of the peace, on demand by an officer of the portion of His Majesty's forces mentioned in a requisition of emergency, or by an officer of the Army Council authorized in this behalf, and on production of the requisition, shall issue his warrant for the provision of such carriages, animals, and vessels as are stated by the officer producing the requisition of emergency to be required for the purpose mentioned in the requisition ; the warrant shall be executed in the like manner, and all the provisions of this Act as to the provision or furnishing of carriages and animals, including those respecting fines on officers, non-commissioned officers, justices, constables, or owners of carriages or animals, shall apply in like manner as in the case where a justice issues, in pursuance of the foregoing provisions of this Act, a warrant for the provision of carriages and animals, and shall apply to vessels as if the expression carriages included vessels.

(4.) The Army Council shall cause due payment to be made for carriages, animals, and vessels furnished in pursuance of this section, and any difference respecting the amount of payment for any carriage, animal or vessel shall be determined by a county court judge having jurisdiction in any place in which such carriage, animal, or vessel was furnished or through which it travelled in pursuance of the requisition.

(5.) Canal, river, or lock tolls are hereby declared not to be demandable for vessels while employed in any service in pursuance of this section, or returning therefrom. And any toll collector who demands or receives toll in contravention of this exemption shall on summary conviction be liable to a fine not exceeding five pounds nor less than ten shillings.

(6.) A requisition of emergency, purported to be issued in pursuance of this section, and to be signed by an officer therein stated to be authorized in accordance with this section, shall be evidence, until the contrary is proved, of its being duly issued and signed in pursuance of this Act, and if delivered to an officer of His Majesty's forces or of the Army Council shall be a sufficient authority to such officer to demand carriages, animals, and vessels in pursuance of this section, and when produced by such officer shall be conclusive evidence to a justice and constable of the authority of such officer to demand carriages, animals, and vessels in accordance with such requisition ; and it shall be lawful to convey on such carriages, animals, and vessels not only the baggage, provisions, and military stores of the troops mentioned in the requisition of emergency, but also the officers, soldiers, servants, women, children, and other persons of and belonging to the same.

(7.) Whenever a proclamation ordering the Army Reserve to be called out on permanent service or an order for the embodiment of the militia is in force, the order of His Majesty authorizing an officer to issue a requisition of emergency may authorize him to extend such requisition to the provision of carriages, animals, and vessels for the purpose of being purchased, as well as of being hired, on behalf of the Crown.

(8.) Where a justice on demand by an officer and on production of a requisition of emergency, has issued his warrant for the provision of any carriages, animals, or vessels, and any person ordered in pursuance of such warrant to furnish a carriage, animal, or vessel, refuses or neglects to furnish the same according to the Order, then, if a proclamation ordering the Army Reserve to be called out on permanent service, or an Order for the embodiment of the militia is in force, the said officer may seize (and if need be by force) the said carriage, animal, or vessel, and may use the same in like manner as if it had been furnished in pursuance of the Order, but the said person shall be entitled to payment for the same in like manner as if he had duly furnished the same according to the Order.

(9.) The Army Council may, by regulations under the Territorial and Reserve Forces Act, 1907, assign to county associations established under that Act the duty of furnishing, in accordance with the directions of the Army Council, such carriages, animals, and vessels as may be required on mobilization for the regular or auxiliary forces, or any part thereof, and where such regulations are made an officer of a county association shall have the same powers as are by this section conferred on an officer of the Army Council.

SECTION 190.

(40.) The expression " horse " includes a mule, and the provisions of this Act shall apply to any beast of whatever description used for burden or draught or for carrying persons in like manner as if such beast were included in the expression " horse."

APPENDIX II.

Form A.

REQUISITION OF EMERGENCY.

(Army Form A. 2029.)

REQUISITION OF EMERGENCY (UNDER THE ARMY ACT, s. 115) FOR THE PROVISION OF CARRIAGES, ANIMALS AND VESSELS FOR THE PURPOSE OF COMPLETING THE WAR ESTABLISHMENT OF HIS MAJESTY'S FORCES.

[*Requisition to be filled in and signed by General or Field Officer authorized to issue it, or, under s. 171 of the Army Act, by a Staff Officer who is authorized to act on behalf of those officers, and shall be expressed as signing on their behalf.*]

Whereas His Majesty in pursuance of Section 115 of the Army Act has by Order dated _____
and signified by_____
a Secretary of State been pleased to order and authorize any General or Field Officer Commanding His Majesty's Regular Forces in any military district or place in the United Kingdom, to issue a requisition of emergency under the said section and to order and authorize any such officer to extend such requisition to the provision of carriages, animals and vessels for the purpose of being purchased, as well as being hired, on behalf of the Crown.

Now, therefore, I, being a General [Field] Officer, Commanding His Majesty's Regular Forces in _____
hereby require the Justices of the Peace to issue their warrant for the provision of carriages, animals and vessels, which may be demanded by authorized officers, in a fit state for use for the purpose of completing the War Establishment of His Majesty's Forces.

Signature _____

To the Justices of the _____

Place_____

Date _____

Form B.

DEMAND ON THE JUSTICE.

DEMAND TO JUSTICE FOR ISSUE OF WARRANT (UNDER THE ARMY ACT, s. 115) FOR THE PROVISION OF CARRIAGES, ANIMALS AND VESSELS FOR THE PURPOSE OF COMPLETING THE WAR ESTABLISHMENT OF HIS MAJESTY'S FORCES.

[*Demand to be filled in and signed by Officer producing the above requisition of emergency.*]

In pursuance of Section 115 of the Army Act and the requisition of emergency which I produce, I _____ being an Officer of His Majesty's Regular Forces in _____ [being an Officer of His Majesty's Forces at _____], [being an Officer of the Army Council duly authorized in this behalf], [being an Officer of the County Association of _____ duly authorized in this behalf], hereby require you to issue your warrant for the provision within _____ day [hours] of the carriages, animals and vessels mentioned in the attached schedule,* in a fit state for the purpose of completing the War Establishment of His Majesty's Forces.

Signature_____

Place_____

Date _____

---

* This schedule is usually framed for convenience on Army Form A. 2034 (outer sheet).

Form C.
JUSTICE'S WARRANT.

WARRANT (UNDER THE ARMY ACT,'S. 115) FOR THE PROVISION OF CARRIAGES, ANIMALS AND VESSELS FOR THE PURPOSE OF COMPLETING THE WAR ESTABLISHMENT OF HIS MAJESTY'S FORCES.

In the county of _____* Petty Sessional Division of _____
[or borough of _____].
To each and all of the constables of_____

A demand has been made in pursuance of a requisition of emergency produced to me by_____, being an officer of His Majesty's Forces mentioned in the said requisition of emergency [being an officer of the Army Council duly authorized in that behalf], [being an officer of the County Association of _____ duly authorized in that behalf], for the provision, for the purpose of completing the War Establishment of His Majesty's Forces, of the carriages,† animals † and vessels mentioned in the schedule attached to this warrant.

You are therefore hereby commanded, on demand being made to you for the purpose by the said_____, to order the several persons in whose possession or control any such carriages, animals and vessels may be, to furnish the same in a fit state for use for the said purpose.

Dated the _____ day of_____ 19 .

Justice of the Peace for the county [or borough] aforesaid. (L.S).

* In Scotland these words must be struck out, and in Ireland the words " Petty Sessions District of " must be substituted.

† Includes harness and stable gear if required.

Form D.
CONSTABLE'S ORDER.

Order to be signed by the Constable and handed to the Owners.

COUNTERFOIL.	
——	G. R.
Impressment Order to	National Emergency. Impressment Order under Section 115 of the Army Act.
	To_____
Horses and Vehicles, &c., Impressed—	His Majesty having declared that a national emergency has arisen, the horses and vehicles enumerated below are to be impressed for the public service, if found fit (in accordance with Section 115 of the Army Act), and will be paid for on the spot at the market value to be settled by the purchasing officer. Should you not accept the price paid as fair value, you have the right to appeal to the County Court (in Scotland the Sheriff's Court), but you must not hinder the delivery of horses, vehicles, &c. The purchasing officer may claim to purchase such harness and stable gear as he may require with the horse or vehicle. Horses and Vehicles required—
	Place_____
	Date _____

APPENDIX III.
THE PAYMENT ORDER.

Army Book 390.

Counterfoil.

Emergency Payment—Horse and Vehicle Impressment.

This order may be presented to the Command Paymaster or collected through a banker.

To the Command Paymaster _____ Command.

Pay _____

£ _____

The sum of (in words) £ _____

_____ horses @ _____

_____ horses @ _____

_____ vehicles and harness @ _____

_____ vehicles and harness @ _____

on account of _____

Military Stations or Units to which consigned.

£ : : _____ Purchaser.

Pay

£

on account of

For (Unit or Military Station)

APPENDIX IV.

A page from the Census Book A.B. 389.

Name and Occupation of Owner.	Address of Stable.	No. of Horses kept.	No. and description of Horses { allotted { classified*										No. of vehicles kept.	Turnouts { allotted { classified*				Water Carts.	Nearest Railway Station.	Unit to which allotted.	Name of Purchasing Officer.	Remarks.
			R.		L.D.		H.D.		P.		Total.		2 wheel.		4 wheel.						
			1	2	1	2							Loads 5-10 cwts.	Loads 10 cwt. or over.	Loads 15 cwt. to 25 cwt.	Loads 25 cwt. or over.					

* This sheet may be used either for *purchasers'* returns, when the word "classified" should be crossed out, or as *census* returns, when the word "allotted" should be crossed out.

Army Form A. 2034.
(Outer Sheet.)

APPENDIX V.

Schedule of Horses to be Impressed.

HORSE AND VEHICLE PURCHASE ON MOBILIZATION.

(To be used for issue to purchasers, detailing the animals and turnouts they are to purchase.   A.B. 389 may be used in lieu if preferred.)

Purchaser's name _____

Unit or Military station
  for which purchase is } _____
  to be made.

No. of Horses to be purchased—
  Riding, Cavalry   ... _____
  Riding, Yeomanry or }
    Mounted Infantry } _____
  Artillery light draught _____
  Transport   „   „   _____
  Heavy draught   ... _____
  Pack   ...   . _____
              Total   ... _____

Turnouts—
  2-wheeled { 5 to 10 cwt. (with ___ horses)_____
             { 10 cwt. or over (with ____ horses) _____
  4-wheeled { 15 cwt. to 25 cwt. (with ___ horses) _____
             { 25 cwt. or over (with ____ horses) _____
  Watercarts (with _____ horse)_____

Bicycles _____

Mechanically Propelled Vehicles :—
  Motor Bicycles _____
    „   Tricycles _____
    „   Cars _____   •
    „   'Buses, including :—
         Char-a-bancs :—(a) to carry up to 19 persons _____
                        (b)   „   20 persons and over_____
  Suitable for transport :—
    Tractors registered under Heavy Motor Car Order _____
    Lorries or Motor Wagons :—
      Steam, carrying 4 to 6 tons _____
      Petrol,   „   10 to 20 cwt._____
        „   „   1 to 4 tons _____
        „   „   4 tons and over _____

Trucks, wagons or trailers fitted to be drawn by Tractors }
     or Lorries—2 to 5 tons carrying capacity   } _____

(B 2481)   Wt. w. 4333—780   1000   11/13   H & S

ND - #0536 - 270225 - C0 - 245/155/2 - PB - 9781908487605 - Matt Lamination